50 Easy Indian Curry Recipes for Home

By: Kelly Johnson

Table of Contents

- Butter Chicken (Murgh Makhani)
- Chicken Tikka Masala
- Chana Masala (Chickpea Curry)
- Aloo Gobi (Potato and Cauliflower Curry)
- Paneer Butter Masala (Paneer Makhani)
- Palak Paneer (Spinach and Paneer Curry)
- Dal Tadka (Tempered Lentils)
- Rajma Masala (Kidney Bean Curry)
- Bhindi Masala (Okra Curry)
- Baingan Bharta (Smoky Eggplant Curry)
- Malai Kofta (Creamy Vegetable Balls)
- Chicken Korma
- Rogan Josh (Kashmiri Lamb Curry)
- Vegetable Jalfrezi
- Mushroom Masala
- Methi Chicken (Chicken with Fenugreek Leaves)
- Pav Bhaji (Spiced Vegetable Mash)
- Egg Curry
- Aloo Palak (Potato and Spinach Curry)
- Chicken Curry
- Fish Curry
- Kadhi Pakora (Yogurt Curry with Fritters)
- Matar Paneer (Peas and Paneer Curry)
- Prawn Curry
- Chicken Saag (Chicken with Spinach)
- Dhaba Style Chicken Curry
- Keema Matar (Minced Meat and Peas Curry)
- Dum Aloo (Potatoes in Spicy Gravy)
- Fish Tikka Masala
- Tofu Tikka Masala
- Vegetable Korma
- Egg Masala
- Chicken Vindaloo
- Lauki Kofta (Bottle Gourd Dumplings in Gravy)
- Baingan Ka Salan (Eggplant Curry in Peanut Sauce)

- Methi Malai Paneer (Paneer in Fenugreek Cream Sauce)
- Chicken Do Pyaza (Chicken Curry with Double Onions)
- Achari Chicken (Pickled Spice Chicken Curry)
- Dum Paneer Kali Mirch (Paneer in Black Pepper Sauce)
- Mutton Curry
- Coconut Chicken Curry
- Jackfruit Curry (Kathal Ki Sabzi)
- Bhuna Chicken (Dry Chicken Curry)
- Shahi Paneer (Royal Paneer Curry)
- Amritsari Chole (Punjabi Style Chickpea Curry)
- Kadai Paneer (Paneer and Bell Pepper Curry)
- Dahi Wale Aloo (Potatoes in Yogurt Curry)
- Methi Malai Mutter (Fenugreek and Peas in Cream Sauce)
- Pindi Chole (Spicy Chickpea Curry)
- Kofta Curry

Butter Chicken (Murgh Makhani)

Ingredients:

- 500g boneless chicken, cut into bite-sized pieces
- 1 cup plain yogurt
- 2 tablespoons lemon juice
- 1 teaspoon ginger paste
- 1 teaspoon garlic paste
- 1 teaspoon red chili powder
- 1 teaspoon garam masala
- Salt to taste
- 2 tablespoons butter
- 1 tablespoon vegetable oil
- 1 onion, finely chopped
- 2 tomatoes, pureed
- 1 teaspoon cumin powder
- 1 teaspoon coriander powder
- 1/2 teaspoon turmeric powder
- 1/2 cup heavy cream
- 1 tablespoon honey or sugar (optional)
- Fresh coriander leaves for garnish

Instructions:

1. In a bowl, mix together yogurt, lemon juice, ginger paste, garlic paste, red chili powder, garam masala, and salt. Add chicken pieces to this marinade, coat well, and refrigerate for at least 1 hour or overnight.
2. Heat butter and vegetable oil in a pan over medium heat. Add chopped onions and sauté until golden brown.
3. Add the marinated chicken along with any remaining marinade to the pan. Cook until the chicken is no longer pink, stirring occasionally, for about 8-10 minutes.
4. Add tomato puree, cumin powder, coriander powder, and turmeric powder to the chicken. Mix well and cook for another 5 minutes.
5. Reduce the heat to low and add heavy cream to the chicken. Stir gently to combine and simmer for 5 minutes.
6. Taste the sauce and adjust the seasoning if needed. If you prefer a sweeter taste, add honey or sugar at this point.

7. Garnish with fresh coriander leaves before serving.
8. Serve hot with naan, rice, or roti.

Enjoy your homemade Butter Chicken!

Chicken Tikka Masala

Ingredients:

- 500g boneless chicken, cut into bite-sized pieces
- 1 cup plain yogurt
- 2 tablespoons lemon juice
- 1 teaspoon ginger paste
- 1 teaspoon garlic paste
- 1 teaspoon red chili powder
- 1 teaspoon ground cumin
- 1 teaspoon ground coriander
- 1/2 teaspoon turmeric powder
- Salt to taste
- 2 tablespoons vegetable oil
- 1 onion, finely chopped
- 2 tomatoes, pureed
- 1 tablespoon tomato paste
- 1 teaspoon garam masala
- 1/2 cup heavy cream
- Fresh coriander leaves for garnish

Instructions:

1. In a bowl, mix together yogurt, lemon juice, ginger paste, garlic paste, red chili powder, ground cumin, ground coriander, turmeric powder, and salt. Add chicken pieces to this marinade, coat well, and refrigerate for at least 1 hour or overnight.
2. Preheat the oven to 200°C (400°F). Thread the marinated chicken pieces onto skewers and place them on a baking tray lined with parchment paper. Bake for 15-20 minutes or until the chicken is cooked through and slightly charred.
3. In a large pan, heat vegetable oil over medium heat. Add chopped onions and sauté until golden brown.
4. Add tomato puree, tomato paste, and garam masala to the onions. Cook for 5 minutes, stirring occasionally.
5. Add the cooked chicken pieces to the tomato mixture. Stir well to coat the chicken with the sauce.
6. Pour in the heavy cream and simmer for another 5 minutes.
7. Taste the sauce and adjust the seasoning if needed.

8. Garnish with fresh coriander leaves before serving.
9. Serve hot with rice or naan.

Enjoy your homemade Chicken Tikka Masala!

Chana Masala (Chickpea Curry)

Ingredients:

- 2 cups cooked chickpeas (or 2 cans, drained and rinsed)
- 2 tablespoons vegetable oil
- 1 onion, finely chopped
- 2 tomatoes, finely chopped or pureed
- 1 tablespoon ginger paste
- 1 tablespoon garlic paste
- 1 green chili, finely chopped (optional)
- 1 teaspoon cumin seeds
- 1 teaspoon ground coriander
- 1 teaspoon ground cumin
- 1 teaspoon turmeric powder
- 1/2 teaspoon red chili powder
- 1/2 teaspoon garam masala
- Salt to taste
- 1 tablespoon dried fenugreek leaves (kasuri methi), crushed (optional)
- Fresh coriander leaves for garnish
- Lemon wedges for serving

Instructions:

1. Heat vegetable oil in a large pan over medium heat. Add cumin seeds and let them splutter.
2. Add chopped onions and sauté until golden brown.
3. Add ginger paste, garlic paste, and green chili (if using). Sauté for another minute.
4. Add chopped tomatoes (or puree) to the pan. Cook until the tomatoes are soft and oil starts to separate from the mixture, about 5-7 minutes.
5. Add ground coriander, ground cumin, turmeric powder, red chili powder, and salt to the tomato mixture. Cook for 2-3 minutes, stirring continuously.
6. Add cooked chickpeas to the pan and mix well with the spice mixture.
7. Add water as needed to achieve the desired consistency. Simmer for 10-15 minutes to allow the flavors to meld together.
8. Sprinkle garam masala and crushed dried fenugreek leaves (if using) over the curry. Stir well.

9. Taste and adjust the seasoning if needed.
10. Garnish with fresh coriander leaves before serving.
11. Serve hot with rice or naan, and lemon wedges on the side.

Enjoy your homemade Chana Masala!

Aloo Gobi (Potato and Cauliflower Curry)

Ingredients:

- 1 medium cauliflower, cut into florets
- 2 medium potatoes, peeled and diced
- 2 tablespoons vegetable oil
- 1 teaspoon cumin seeds
- 1 onion, finely chopped
- 2 tomatoes, finely chopped or pureed
- 1 tablespoon ginger paste
- 1 tablespoon garlic paste
- 1 green chili, finely chopped (optional)
- 1 teaspoon ground turmeric
- 1 teaspoon ground cumin
- 1 teaspoon ground coriander
- 1/2 teaspoon red chili powder
- Salt to taste
- Fresh coriander leaves for garnish

Instructions:

1. Heat vegetable oil in a large pan over medium heat. Add cumin seeds and let them splutter.
2. Add chopped onions and sauté until golden brown.
3. Add ginger paste, garlic paste, and green chili (if using). Sauté for another minute.
4. Add chopped tomatoes (or puree) to the pan. Cook until the tomatoes are soft and oil starts to separate from the mixture, about 5-7 minutes.
5. Add ground turmeric, ground cumin, ground coriander, red chili powder, and salt to the tomato mixture. Cook for 2-3 minutes, stirring continuously.
6. Add diced potatoes to the pan and mix well with the spice mixture. Cook for 5 minutes.
7. Add cauliflower florets to the pan and mix well to coat them with the spice mixture.
8. Cover the pan and cook on low heat for about 15-20 minutes, or until the potatoes and cauliflower are tender, stirring occasionally.

9. Once the vegetables are cooked through, uncover the pan and cook for another 5 minutes to allow excess moisture to evaporate.
10. Taste and adjust the seasoning if needed.
11. Garnish with fresh coriander leaves before serving.
12. Serve hot with rice or roti.

Enjoy your homemade Aloo Gobi!

Paneer Butter Masala (Paneer Makhani)

Ingredients:

- 250g paneer, cut into cubes
- 2 tablespoons butter
- 1 tablespoon vegetable oil
- 1 onion, finely chopped
- 2 tomatoes, finely chopped or pureed
- 1 tablespoon ginger paste
- 1 tablespoon garlic paste
- 1 green chili, finely chopped (optional)
- 1 teaspoon Kashmiri red chili powder (for color)
- 1 teaspoon ground cumin
- 1 teaspoon ground coriander
- 1/2 teaspoon turmeric powder
- 1/2 teaspoon garam masala
- Salt to taste
- 1/4 cup heavy cream
- 1 tablespoon honey or sugar (optional)
- Fresh coriander leaves for garnish

Instructions:

1. Heat butter and vegetable oil in a large pan over medium heat.
2. Add chopped onions and sauté until golden brown.
3. Add ginger paste, garlic paste, and green chili (if using). Sauté for another minute.
4. Add chopped tomatoes (or puree) to the pan. Cook until the tomatoes are soft and oil starts to separate from the mixture, about 5-7 minutes.
5. Add Kashmiri red chili powder, ground cumin, ground coriander, turmeric powder, and salt to the tomato mixture. Cook for 2-3 minutes, stirring continuously.
6. Add paneer cubes to the pan and mix well with the spice mixture. Cook for 2-3 minutes to allow the paneer to absorb the flavors.
7. Pour in heavy cream and garam masala. Stir gently to combine.
8. If you prefer a sweeter taste, add honey or sugar at this point.
9. Simmer the curry for another 5 minutes, stirring occasionally.
10. Taste and adjust the seasoning if needed.

11. Garnish with fresh coriander leaves before serving.
12. Serve hot with rice or naan.

Enjoy your homemade Paneer Butter Masala!

Palak Paneer (Spinach and Paneer Curry)

Ingredients:

- 250g paneer, cut into cubes
- 500g fresh spinach leaves, washed and chopped
- 2 tablespoons ghee or vegetable oil
- 1 onion, finely chopped
- 2 tomatoes, finely chopped or pureed
- 1 tablespoon ginger paste
- 1 tablespoon garlic paste
- 1 green chili, finely chopped (optional)
- 1 teaspoon cumin seeds
- 1 teaspoon ground coriander
- 1/2 teaspoon turmeric powder
- 1/2 teaspoon garam masala
- Salt to taste
- 1/4 cup heavy cream (optional)
- Fresh coriander leaves for garnish

Instructions:

1. Heat ghee or vegetable oil in a large pan over medium heat.
2. Add cumin seeds and let them splutter.
3. Add chopped onions and sauté until golden brown.
4. Add ginger paste, garlic paste, and green chili (if using). Sauté for another minute.
5. Add chopped tomatoes (or puree) to the pan. Cook until the tomatoes are soft and oil starts to separate from the mixture, about 5-7 minutes.
6. Add ground coriander, turmeric powder, and salt to the tomato mixture. Stir well and cook for 2-3 minutes.
7. Add chopped spinach leaves to the pan. Stir and cook until the spinach wilts down, about 5 minutes.
8. Allow the mixture to cool slightly, then blend it into a smooth paste using a blender or immersion blender.
9. Return the spinach mixture to the pan. Add paneer cubes and garam masala. Stir gently to combine.
10. If using, pour in heavy cream and stir well.

11. Simmer the curry for another 5 minutes, stirring occasionally.
12. Taste and adjust the seasoning if needed.
13. Garnish with fresh coriander leaves before serving.
14. Serve hot with rice or naan.

Enjoy your homemade Palak Paneer!

Dal Tadka (Tempered Lentils)

Ingredients:

- 1 cup yellow split lentils (moong dal) or red lentils (masoor dal)
- 4 cups water
- 1 teaspoon turmeric powder
- Salt to taste

For Tempering (Tadka):

- 2 tablespoons ghee or vegetable oil
- 1 teaspoon cumin seeds
- 1 onion, finely chopped
- 2 tomatoes, finely chopped or pureed
- 1 tablespoon ginger paste
- 1 tablespoon garlic paste
- 1 green chili, finely chopped (optional)
- 1 teaspoon ground coriander
- 1/2 teaspoon red chili powder
- 1/2 teaspoon garam masala
- Fresh coriander leaves for garnish

Instructions:

1. Rinse the lentils under cold water until the water runs clear. Drain well.
2. In a large saucepan, combine lentils, water, turmeric powder, and salt. Bring to a boil over medium-high heat.
3. Once boiling, reduce the heat to low and simmer partially covered for about 20-25 minutes or until the lentils are soft and cooked through. Stir occasionally to prevent sticking.
4. While the lentils are cooking, prepare the tempering (tadka). Heat ghee or vegetable oil in a small pan over medium heat.
5. Add cumin seeds to the hot oil and let them splutter.
6. Add chopped onions and sauté until golden brown.
7. Add ginger paste, garlic paste, and green chili (if using). Sauté for another minute.

8. Add chopped tomatoes (or puree) to the pan. Cook until the tomatoes are soft and oil starts to separate from the mixture, about 5-7 minutes.
9. Add ground coriander, red chili powder, and garam masala to the tomato mixture. Stir well and cook for 2-3 minutes.
10. Once the lentils are cooked, add the prepared tempering (tadka) to the lentils. Stir well to combine.
11. Simmer the dal for another 5 minutes, stirring occasionally.
12. Taste and adjust the seasoning if needed.
13. Garnish with fresh coriander leaves before serving.
14. Serve hot with rice or roti.

Enjoy your homemade Dal Tadka!

Rajma Masala (Kidney Bean Curry)

Ingredients:

- 1 cup dried kidney beans (rajma), soaked overnight or for at least 8 hours
- 4 cups water
- 2 tablespoons vegetable oil
- 1 onion, finely chopped
- 2 tomatoes, finely chopped or pureed
- 1 tablespoon ginger paste
- 1 tablespoon garlic paste
- 1 green chili, finely chopped (optional)
- 1 teaspoon cumin seeds
- 1 teaspoon ground coriander
- 1/2 teaspoon turmeric powder
- 1/2 teaspoon red chili powder
- 1/2 teaspoon garam masala
- Salt to taste
- Fresh coriander leaves for garnish

Instructions:

1. Rinse the soaked kidney beans under cold water until the water runs clear. Drain well.
2. In a large pot, combine kidney beans and 4 cups of water. Bring to a boil over medium-high heat.
3. Once boiling, reduce the heat to low and simmer partially covered for about 45-60 minutes or until the kidney beans are soft and cooked through. Stir occasionally and add more water if needed.
4. While the kidney beans are cooking, prepare the masala. Heat vegetable oil in a large pan over medium heat.
5. Add cumin seeds to the hot oil and let them splutter.
6. Add chopped onions and sauté until golden brown.
7. Add ginger paste, garlic paste, and green chili (if using). Sauté for another minute.
8. Add chopped tomatoes (or puree) to the pan. Cook until the tomatoes are soft and oil starts to separate from the mixture, about 5-7 minutes.

9. Add ground coriander, turmeric powder, red chili powder, and salt to the tomato mixture. Stir well and cook for 2-3 minutes.
10. Once the kidney beans are cooked, add the prepared masala to the pot. Stir well to combine.
11. Add garam masala to the pot and simmer the curry for another 10-15 minutes, stirring occasionally.
12. Taste and adjust the seasoning if needed.
13. Garnish with fresh coriander leaves before serving.
14. Serve hot with rice or roti.

Enjoy your homemade Rajma Masala!

Bhindi Masala (Okra Curry)

Ingredients:

- 500g fresh okra (bhindi), washed, dried, and cut into 1-inch pieces
- 2 tablespoons vegetable oil
- 1 teaspoon cumin seeds
- 1 onion, finely chopped
- 2 tomatoes, finely chopped or pureed
- 1 tablespoon ginger paste
- 1 tablespoon garlic paste
- 1 green chili, finely chopped (optional)
- 1 teaspoon ground coriander
- 1/2 teaspoon turmeric powder
- 1/2 teaspoon red chili powder
- 1/2 teaspoon garam masala
- Salt to taste
- Fresh coriander leaves for garnish

Instructions:

1. Heat vegetable oil in a large pan over medium heat.
2. Add cumin seeds to the hot oil and let them splutter.
3. Add chopped onions and sauté until golden brown.
4. Add ginger paste, garlic paste, and green chili (if using). Sauté for another minute.
5. Add chopped tomatoes (or puree) to the pan. Cook until the tomatoes are soft and oil starts to separate from the mixture, about 5-7 minutes.
6. Add ground coriander, turmeric powder, red chili powder, and salt to the tomato mixture. Stir well and cook for 2-3 minutes.
7. Add chopped okra to the pan. Stir well to coat the okra with the spice mixture.
8. Cover the pan and cook on low heat for about 10-15 minutes, or until the okra is tender, stirring occasionally.
9. Once the okra is cooked, sprinkle garam masala over the curry. Stir gently to combine.
10. Taste and adjust the seasoning if needed.
11. Garnish with fresh coriander leaves before serving.
12. Serve hot with rice or roti.

Enjoy your homemade Bhindi Masala!

Baingan Bharta (Smoky Eggplant Curry)

Ingredients:

- 2 large eggplants (baingan)
- 2 tablespoons vegetable oil
- 1 onion, finely chopped
- 2 tomatoes, finely chopped
- 1 tablespoon ginger paste
- 1 tablespoon garlic paste
- 1 green chili, finely chopped (optional)
- 1 teaspoon cumin seeds
- 1 teaspoon ground coriander
- 1/2 teaspoon turmeric powder
- 1/2 teaspoon red chili powder
- 1/2 teaspoon garam masala
- Salt to taste
- Fresh coriander leaves for garnish

Instructions:

1. Preheat the oven to 200°C (400°F). Pierce the eggplants with a fork in several places. Place them on a baking sheet and roast in the preheated oven for 30-40 minutes, or until the skin is charred and the flesh is soft. Alternatively, you can roast the eggplants over an open flame on a gas stove or grill until charred and tender. Allow the roasted eggplants to cool slightly, then peel off the charred skin and discard it. Mash the roasted eggplant flesh using a fork or potato masher. Set aside.
2. Heat vegetable oil in a large pan over medium heat.
3. Add cumin seeds to the hot oil and let them splutter.
4. Add chopped onions and sauté until golden brown.
5. Add ginger paste, garlic paste, and green chili (if using). Sauté for another minute.
6. Add chopped tomatoes to the pan. Cook until the tomatoes are soft and oil starts to separate from the mixture, about 5-7 minutes.
7. Add ground coriander, turmeric powder, red chili powder, and salt to the tomato mixture. Stir well and cook for 2-3 minutes.
8. Add mashed eggplant to the pan. Stir well to combine with the spice mixture.

9. Cook the mixture for another 5-7 minutes, stirring occasionally.
10. Sprinkle garam masala over the curry. Stir gently to combine.
11. Taste and adjust the seasoning if needed.
12. Garnish with fresh coriander leaves before serving.
13. Serve hot with rice or roti.

Enjoy your homemade Baingan Bharta!

Malai Kofta (Creamy Vegetable Balls)
Ingredients:

For the Kofta:

- 2 large potatoes, boiled and mashed
- 1 cup mixed vegetables (carrots, peas, beans), finely chopped and steamed
- 1/4 cup paneer, grated
- 2 tablespoons corn flour or all-purpose flour
- 1 teaspoon ginger paste
- 1 teaspoon garlic paste
- 1 green chili, finely chopped (optional)
- 1/2 teaspoon garam masala
- Salt to taste
- Vegetable oil for frying

For the Gravy:

- 2 tablespoons ghee or vegetable oil
- 1 onion, finely chopped
- 2 tomatoes, finely chopped or pureed
- 1 tablespoon ginger paste
- 1 tablespoon garlic paste
- 1 green chili, finely chopped (optional)
- 1 teaspoon ground coriander
- 1/2 teaspoon turmeric powder
- 1/2 teaspoon red chili powder
- 1/2 teaspoon garam masala
- 1/2 cup cashew nuts, soaked in warm water for 30 minutes and ground into a smooth paste
- 1/4 cup heavy cream
- Salt to taste
- Fresh coriander leaves for garnish

Instructions:

1. To make the kofta, in a large mixing bowl, combine mashed potatoes, steamed mixed vegetables, grated paneer, corn flour or all-purpose flour, ginger paste,

garlic paste, green chili (if using), garam masala, and salt. Mix well until everything is well combined.
2. Divide the mixture into equal-sized portions and shape them into round balls (koftas).
3. Heat vegetable oil in a deep frying pan over medium heat. Once the oil is hot, carefully add the koftas in batches and fry until golden brown and crispy on all sides. Remove them from the oil using a slotted spoon and drain on paper towels. Set aside.
4. To make the gravy, heat ghee or vegetable oil in a large pan over medium heat.
5. Add chopped onions and sauté until golden brown.
6. Add ginger paste, garlic paste, and green chili (if using). Sauté for another minute.
7. Add chopped tomatoes (or puree) to the pan. Cook until the tomatoes are soft and oil starts to separate from the mixture, about 5-7 minutes.
8. Add ground coriander, turmeric powder, red chili powder, and garam masala to the tomato mixture. Stir well and cook for 2-3 minutes.
9. Add ground cashew paste to the pan. Mix well to combine with the spice mixture.
10. Pour in heavy cream and stir well. Let the gravy simmer for 2-3 minutes.
11. Add salt to taste and adjust the consistency of the gravy by adding water if needed.
12. Gently add the fried koftas to the gravy and simmer for another 5-7 minutes, allowing the koftas to absorb the flavors of the gravy.
13. Garnish with fresh coriander leaves before serving.
14. Serve hot with rice or naan.

Enjoy your homemade Malai Kofta!

Chicken Korma

Ingredients:

- 500g boneless chicken, cut into bite-sized pieces
- 2 tablespoons vegetable oil
- 1 onion, finely chopped
- 2 tomatoes, finely chopped or pureed
- 1 tablespoon ginger paste
- 1 tablespoon garlic paste
- 1 green chili, finely chopped (optional)
- 1/2 cup plain yogurt
- 1/4 cup cashew nuts, soaked in warm water for 30 minutes and ground into a smooth paste
- 1/4 cup almond flour or ground almonds
- 1 teaspoon ground coriander
- 1/2 teaspoon ground cumin
- 1/2 teaspoon turmeric powder
- 1/2 teaspoon red chili powder
- 1/2 teaspoon garam masala
- Salt to taste
- 1/4 cup heavy cream
- Fresh coriander leaves for garnish

Instructions:

1. Heat vegetable oil in a large pan over medium heat.
2. Add chopped onions and sauté until golden brown.
3. Add ginger paste, garlic paste, and green chili (if using). Sauté for another minute.
4. Add chopped tomatoes (or puree) to the pan. Cook until the tomatoes are soft and oil starts to separate from the mixture, about 5-7 minutes.
5. In a bowl, whisk together plain yogurt, ground cashew paste, almond flour (or ground almonds), ground coriander, ground cumin, turmeric powder, red chili powder, garam masala, and salt.
6. Add the yogurt mixture to the pan. Stir well to combine with the onion-tomato mixture.
7. Add chicken pieces to the pan. Mix well to coat the chicken with the sauce.

8. Cover the pan and simmer on low heat for about 20-25 minutes, or until the chicken is cooked through and tender, stirring occasionally.
9. Once the chicken is cooked, pour in heavy cream and stir well. Let the korma simmer for another 2-3 minutes.
10. Taste and adjust the seasoning if needed.
11. Garnish with fresh coriander leaves before serving.
12. Serve hot with rice, naan, or roti.

Enjoy your homemade Chicken Korma!

Rogan Josh (Kashmiri Lamb Curry)

Ingredients:

- 500g lamb, cut into bite-sized pieces
- 2 tablespoons vegetable oil or ghee
- 2 onions, finely chopped
- 2 tomatoes, finely chopped or pureed
- 1 tablespoon ginger paste
- 1 tablespoon garlic paste
- 1 green chili, finely chopped (optional)
- 1/2 cup plain yogurt
- 1 teaspoon ground coriander
- 1/2 teaspoon ground cumin
- 1/2 teaspoon ground cardamom
- 1/2 teaspoon ground cinnamon
- 1/2 teaspoon ground cloves
- 1/2 teaspoon ground fennel seeds
- 1/2 teaspoon turmeric powder
- 1/2 teaspoon red chili powder
- Salt to taste
- 1/2 cup water
- Fresh coriander leaves for garnish

Instructions:

1. Heat vegetable oil or ghee in a large pan over medium heat.
2. Add chopped onions and sauté until golden brown.
3. Add ginger paste, garlic paste, and green chili (if using). Sauté for another minute.
4. Add chopped tomatoes (or puree) to the pan. Cook until the tomatoes are soft and oil starts to separate from the mixture, about 5-7 minutes.
5. In a bowl, whisk together plain yogurt, ground coriander, ground cumin, ground cardamom, ground cinnamon, ground cloves, ground fennel seeds, turmeric powder, red chili powder, and salt.
6. Add the yogurt mixture to the pan. Stir well to combine with the onion-tomato mixture.
7. Add lamb pieces to the pan. Mix well to coat the lamb with the sauce.

8. Add water to the pan, cover, and simmer on low heat for about 60-90 minutes, or until the lamb is tender and the sauce has thickened, stirring occasionally.
9. Once the lamb is cooked, taste and adjust the seasoning if needed.
10. Garnish with fresh coriander leaves before serving.
11. Serve hot with rice, naan, or roti.

Enjoy your homemade Rogan Josh!

Vegetable Jalfrezi

Ingredients:

- 2 tablespoons vegetable oil
- 1 onion, thinly sliced
- 1 bell pepper (capsicum), thinly sliced
- 1 carrot, thinly sliced
- 1 cup cauliflower florets
- 1 cup broccoli florets
- 1 cup green beans, trimmed and cut into 1-inch pieces
- 1 cup paneer (Indian cottage cheese), cubed (optional)
- 2 tomatoes, finely chopped or pureed
- 1 tablespoon ginger paste
- 1 tablespoon garlic paste
- 1 green chili, finely chopped (optional)
- 1 teaspoon ground coriander
- 1/2 teaspoon ground cumin
- 1/2 teaspoon turmeric powder
- 1/2 teaspoon red chili powder
- 1/2 teaspoon garam masala
- Salt to taste
- Fresh coriander leaves for garnish

Instructions:

1. Heat vegetable oil in a large pan over medium heat.
2. Add thinly sliced onions and sauté until golden brown.
3. Add ginger paste, garlic paste, and green chili (if using). Sauté for another minute.
4. Add thinly sliced bell pepper, carrot, cauliflower florets, broccoli florets, and green beans to the pan. Stir-fry for 5-7 minutes or until the vegetables are slightly tender.
5. Add chopped tomatoes (or puree) to the pan. Cook until the tomatoes are soft and oil starts to separate from the mixture, about 5-7 minutes.
6. Add ground coriander, ground cumin, turmeric powder, red chili powder, garam masala, and salt to the pan. Stir well to combine with the vegetables.

7. If using paneer, add cubed paneer to the pan and gently mix with the vegetables and spices.
8. Cover the pan and simmer on low heat for another 5-7 minutes, allowing the flavors to meld together.
9. Taste and adjust the seasoning if needed.
10. Garnish with fresh coriander leaves before serving.
11. Serve hot with rice, naan, or roti.

Enjoy your homemade Vegetable Jalfrezi!

Mushroom Masala

Ingredients:

- 500g mushrooms, sliced
- 2 tablespoons vegetable oil
- 1 onion, finely chopped
- 2 tomatoes, finely chopped or pureed
- 1 tablespoon ginger paste
- 1 tablespoon garlic paste
- 1 green chili, finely chopped (optional)
- 1 teaspoon ground coriander
- 1/2 teaspoon ground cumin
- 1/2 teaspoon turmeric powder
- 1/2 teaspoon red chili powder
- 1/2 teaspoon garam masala
- Salt to taste
- Fresh coriander leaves for garnish

Instructions:

1. Heat vegetable oil in a large pan over medium heat.
2. Add chopped onions and sauté until golden brown.
3. Add ginger paste, garlic paste, and green chili (if using). Sauté for another minute.
4. Add chopped tomatoes (or puree) to the pan. Cook until the tomatoes are soft and oil starts to separate from the mixture, about 5-7 minutes.
5. Add sliced mushrooms to the pan. Stir well to combine with the onion-tomato mixture.
6. Add ground coriander, ground cumin, turmeric powder, red chili powder, and salt to the pan. Stir well to coat the mushrooms with the spices.
7. Cover the pan and simmer on low heat for about 10-15 minutes, or until the mushrooms are cooked through and tender, stirring occasionally.
8. Once the mushrooms are cooked, sprinkle garam masala over the curry. Stir gently to combine.
9. Taste and adjust the seasoning if needed.
10. Garnish with fresh coriander leaves before serving.
11. Serve hot with rice, naan, or roti.

Enjoy your homemade Mushroom Masala!

Methi Chicken (Chicken with Fenugreek Leaves)

Ingredients:

- 500g chicken, cut into bite-sized pieces
- 2 cups fresh fenugreek leaves (methi), washed and finely chopped
- 2 tablespoons vegetable oil
- 1 onion, finely chopped
- 2 tomatoes, finely chopped or pureed
- 1 tablespoon ginger paste
- 1 tablespoon garlic paste
- 1 green chili, finely chopped (optional)
- 1 teaspoon ground coriander
- 1/2 teaspoon ground cumin
- 1/2 teaspoon turmeric powder
- 1/2 teaspoon red chili powder
- 1/2 teaspoon garam masala
- Salt to taste
- Fresh coriander leaves for garnish

Instructions:

1. Heat vegetable oil in a large pan over medium heat.
2. Add chopped onions and sauté until golden brown.
3. Add ginger paste, garlic paste, and green chili (if using). Sauté for another minute.
4. Add chopped tomatoes (or puree) to the pan. Cook until the tomatoes are soft and oil starts to separate from the mixture, about 5-7 minutes.
5. Add chicken pieces to the pan. Mix well to combine with the onion-tomato mixture.
6. Add ground coriander, ground cumin, turmeric powder, red chili powder, and salt to the pan. Stir well to coat the chicken with the spices.
7. Cover the pan and cook on low heat for about 15-20 minutes, or until the chicken is almost cooked through, stirring occasionally.
8. Add finely chopped fenugreek leaves (methi) to the pan. Mix well with the chicken and spices.
9. Cover the pan again and cook for another 10-15 minutes, or until the chicken is fully cooked and the fenugreek leaves are wilted and tender, stirring occasionally.

10. Once the chicken is cooked, sprinkle garam masala over the curry. Stir gently to combine.
11. Taste and adjust the seasoning if needed.
12. Garnish with fresh coriander leaves before serving.
13. Serve hot with rice, naan, or roti.

Enjoy your homemade Methi Chicken!

Pav Bhaji (Spiced Vegetable Mash)

Ingredients:

- 4 medium potatoes, boiled and mashed
- 1 cup cauliflower florets, boiled and mashed
- 1/2 cup green peas, boiled
- 1/2 cup carrots, boiled and mashed
- 1/2 cup bell peppers (capsicum), finely chopped
- 1 large onion, finely chopped
- 2 tomatoes, finely chopped
- 2 green chilies, finely chopped
- 1 tablespoon ginger-garlic paste
- 2 tablespoons butter
- 1 tablespoon pav bhaji masala
- 1 teaspoon red chili powder
- 1/2 teaspoon turmeric powder
- Salt to taste
- Fresh coriander leaves for garnish
- Lemon wedges for serving
- Pav (bread rolls) for serving

Instructions:

1. Heat butter in a large pan or kadai over medium heat.
2. Add finely chopped onions and green chilies. Sauté until onions turn translucent.
3. Add ginger-garlic paste and sauté for another minute until the raw smell disappears.
4. Add finely chopped bell peppers and sauté for 2-3 minutes until they soften.
5. Add finely chopped tomatoes and cook until they turn mushy and the oil starts to separate.
6. Add pav bhaji masala, red chili powder, turmeric powder, and salt. Mix well and cook for 2 minutes.
7. Add mashed potatoes, cauliflower, carrots, and boiled green peas to the pan. Mix everything well until combined.
8. Mash the vegetables using a potato masher or the back of a spoon. Continue mashing until you get a smooth consistency.

9. Add water as needed to adjust the consistency. Simmer the bhaji for 5-10 minutes, stirring occasionally.
10. Once the bhaji reaches the desired consistency, turn off the heat.
11. Garnish with chopped coriander leaves and a dollop of butter.
12. Toast the pav (bread rolls) on a griddle or tawa with a little butter until they are crisp and golden brown.
13. Serve the hot pav bhaji with lemon wedges and additional chopped onions on the side.

Enjoy your homemade Pav Bhaji!

Egg Curry

Ingredients:

- 6 hard-boiled eggs, peeled and halved
- 2 tablespoons vegetable oil
- 1 onion, finely chopped
- 2 tomatoes, finely chopped or pureed
- 1 tablespoon ginger paste
- 1 tablespoon garlic paste
- 1 green chili, finely chopped (optional)
- 1 teaspoon ground coriander
- 1/2 teaspoon ground cumin
- 1/2 teaspoon turmeric powder
- 1/2 teaspoon red chili powder
- 1/2 teaspoon garam masala
- Salt to taste
- Fresh coriander leaves for garnish

Instructions:

1. Heat vegetable oil in a large pan over medium heat.
2. Add chopped onions and sauté until golden brown.
3. Add ginger paste, garlic paste, and green chili (if using). Sauté for another minute.
4. Add chopped tomatoes (or puree) to the pan. Cook until the tomatoes are soft and oil starts to separate from the mixture, about 5-7 minutes.
5. Add ground coriander, ground cumin, turmeric powder, red chili powder, and salt to the pan. Stir well to combine with the onion-tomato mixture.
6. Add 1 cup of water to the pan and bring the mixture to a simmer.
7. Carefully place the halved hard-boiled eggs into the simmering curry, cut side up.
8. Cover the pan and let the curry simmer on low heat for about 10-15 minutes, allowing the flavors to meld together and the eggs to absorb the spices.
9. Once the eggs are heated through and the curry has reached the desired consistency, sprinkle garam masala over the curry. Stir gently to combine.
10. Taste and adjust the seasoning if needed.
11. Garnish with fresh coriander leaves before serving.
12. Serve hot with rice, naan, or roti.

Enjoy your homemade Egg Curry!

Aloo Palak (Potato and Spinach Curry)

Ingredients:

- 3 medium potatoes, peeled and cubed
- 4 cups fresh spinach leaves, washed and chopped
- 2 tablespoons vegetable oil
- 1 teaspoon cumin seeds
- 1 onion, finely chopped
- 1 tablespoon ginger paste
- 1 tablespoon garlic paste
- 2 tomatoes, finely chopped or pureed
- 1 green chili, finely chopped (optional)
- 1 teaspoon ground coriander
- 1/2 teaspoon turmeric powder
- 1/2 teaspoon red chili powder
- 1/2 teaspoon garam masala
- Salt to taste
- Fresh coriander leaves for garnish

Instructions:

1. Boil the cubed potatoes in salted water until they are fork-tender. Drain and set aside.
2. Heat vegetable oil in a large pan over medium heat.
3. Add cumin seeds to the hot oil and let them splutter.
4. Add chopped onions and sauté until golden brown.
5. Add ginger paste, garlic paste, and green chili (if using). Sauté for another minute.
6. Add chopped tomatoes (or puree) to the pan. Cook until the tomatoes are soft and oil starts to separate from the mixture, about 5-7 minutes.
7. Add ground coriander, turmeric powder, red chili powder, and salt to the tomato mixture. Stir well and cook for 2-3 minutes.
8. Add chopped spinach leaves to the pan. Stir well to combine with the tomato mixture. Cook until the spinach wilts down, about 5 minutes.
9. Add boiled potatoes to the pan. Mix well with the spinach and tomato mixture.
10. Cover the pan and simmer on low heat for another 10-15 minutes, allowing the flavors to meld together.

11. Once the potatoes are heated through and the curry has reached the desired consistency, sprinkle garam masala over the curry. Stir gently to combine.
12. Taste and adjust the seasoning if needed.
13. Garnish with fresh coriander leaves before serving.
14. Serve hot with rice, naan, or roti.

Enjoy your homemade Aloo Palak!

Chicken Curry

Ingredients:

- 500g chicken pieces (bone-in or boneless)
- 2 tablespoons vegetable oil
- 1 onion, finely chopped
- 2 tomatoes, finely chopped or pureed
- 1 tablespoon ginger paste
- 1 tablespoon garlic paste
- 1 green chili, finely chopped (optional)
- 1 teaspoon ground coriander
- 1/2 teaspoon ground cumin
- 1/2 teaspoon turmeric powder
- 1/2 teaspoon red chili powder
- 1/2 teaspoon garam masala
- Salt to taste
- Fresh coriander leaves for garnish

Instructions:

1. Heat vegetable oil in a large pan over medium heat.
2. Add chopped onions and sauté until golden brown.
3. Add ginger paste, garlic paste, and green chili (if using). Sauté for another minute.
4. Add chopped tomatoes (or puree) to the pan. Cook until the tomatoes are soft and oil starts to separate from the mixture, about 5-7 minutes.
5. Add ground coriander, ground cumin, turmeric powder, red chili powder, and salt to the pan. Stir well to combine with the onion-tomato mixture.
6. Add chicken pieces to the pan. Mix well to coat the chicken with the spices.
7. Cover the pan and cook on low heat for about 20-25 minutes, or until the chicken is cooked through, stirring occasionally.
8. Once the chicken is cooked, sprinkle garam masala over the curry. Stir gently to combine.
9. Taste and adjust the seasoning if needed.
10. Garnish with fresh coriander leaves before serving.
11. Serve hot with rice, naan, or roti.

Enjoy your homemade Chicken Curry!

Fish Curry

Ingredients:

- 500g fish fillets (such as cod, tilapia, or salmon), cut into pieces
- 2 tablespoons vegetable oil
- 1 onion, finely chopped
- 2 tomatoes, finely chopped or pureed
- 1 tablespoon ginger paste
- 1 tablespoon garlic paste
- 1 green chili, finely chopped (optional)
- 1 teaspoon ground coriander
- 1/2 teaspoon ground cumin
- 1/2 teaspoon turmeric powder
- 1/2 teaspoon red chili powder
- 1/2 teaspoon garam masala
- Salt to taste
- Fresh coriander leaves for garnish

Instructions:

1. Heat vegetable oil in a large pan over medium heat.
2. Add chopped onions and sauté until golden brown.
3. Add ginger paste, garlic paste, and green chili (if using). Sauté for another minute.
4. Add chopped tomatoes (or puree) to the pan. Cook until the tomatoes are soft and oil starts to separate from the mixture, about 5-7 minutes.
5. Add ground coriander, ground cumin, turmeric powder, red chili powder, and salt to the pan. Stir well to combine with the onion-tomato mixture.
6. Add fish pieces to the pan. Mix gently to coat the fish with the spices.
7. Cover the pan and simmer on low heat for about 10-15 minutes, or until the fish is cooked through, stirring occasionally.
8. Once the fish is cooked, sprinkle garam masala over the curry. Stir gently to combine.
9. Taste and adjust the seasoning if needed.
10. Garnish with fresh coriander leaves before serving.
11. Serve hot with rice or naan.

Enjoy your homemade Fish Curry!

Kadhi Pakora (Yogurt Curry with Fritters)

Ingredients:

For Pakoras (Fritters):

- 1 cup gram flour (besan)
- 1 onion, finely chopped
- 1/2 teaspoon cumin seeds
- 1/2 teaspoon red chili powder
- 1/4 teaspoon turmeric powder
- Salt to taste
- Water as needed
- Vegetable oil for frying

For Kadhi (Yogurt Curry):

- 1 cup plain yogurt
- 3 tablespoons gram flour (besan)
- 2 cups water
- 1 tablespoon vegetable oil
- 1 teaspoon cumin seeds
- 1 onion, finely chopped
- 2 green chilies, slit lengthwise
- 1 tablespoon ginger-garlic paste
- 1/2 teaspoon turmeric powder
- 1 teaspoon red chili powder
- 1/2 teaspoon coriander powder
- Salt to taste
- Fresh coriander leaves for garnish

Instructions:

1. To make Pakoras:
    - In a mixing bowl, combine gram flour, chopped onion, cumin seeds, red chili powder, turmeric powder, and salt.
    - Gradually add water to form a thick batter.
    - Heat vegetable oil in a deep frying pan over medium heat.

- Drop small portions of the batter into the hot oil and fry until golden brown and crispy.
- Remove the pakoras from the oil and drain on paper towels. Set aside.

2. To make Kadhi:
    - In a bowl, whisk together plain yogurt and gram flour until smooth.
    - Gradually add water, whisking continuously, to make a smooth mixture.
    - Heat vegetable oil in a large pan over medium heat.
    - Add cumin seeds and let them splutter.
    - Add chopped onions and sauté until golden brown.
    - Add slit green chilies and ginger-garlic paste. Sauté for a minute.
    - Lower the heat and add turmeric powder, red chili powder, coriander powder, and salt. Mix well.
    - Pour the yogurt mixture into the pan while stirring continuously to prevent lumps from forming.
    - Cook the kadhi on low heat, stirring occasionally, until it thickens and comes to a gentle boil. This may take about 15-20 minutes.
    - Once the kadhi has thickened, add the pakoras to the curry. Simmer for another 5-10 minutes.
    - Garnish with fresh coriander leaves before serving.

Serve hot Kadhi Pakora with steamed rice or chapati.

Enjoy your homemade Kadhi Pakora!

Matar Paneer (Peas and Paneer Curry)

Ingredients:

- 200g paneer, cut into cubes
- 1 cup green peas (fresh or frozen)
- 2 tablespoons vegetable oil
- 1 onion, finely chopped
- 2 tomatoes, finely chopped or pureed
- 1 tablespoon ginger paste
- 1 tablespoon garlic paste
- 1 green chili, finely chopped (optional)
- 1 teaspoon ground coriander
- 1/2 teaspoon ground cumin
- 1/2 teaspoon turmeric powder
- 1/2 teaspoon red chili powder
- 1/2 teaspoon garam masala
- Salt to taste
- Fresh coriander leaves for garnish

Instructions:

1. Heat vegetable oil in a large pan over medium heat.
2. Add chopped onions and sauté until golden brown.
3. Add ginger paste, garlic paste, and green chili (if using). Sauté for another minute.
4. Add chopped tomatoes (or puree) to the pan. Cook until the tomatoes are soft and oil starts to separate from the mixture, about 5-7 minutes.
5. Add ground coriander, ground cumin, turmeric powder, red chili powder, and salt to the pan. Stir well to combine with the onion-tomato mixture.
6. Add green peas to the pan. Stir well to coat the peas with the spice mixture.
7. Cover the pan and simmer on low heat for about 5-7 minutes, or until the peas are cooked through, stirring occasionally.
8. Add paneer cubes to the pan. Gently mix with the peas and spices.
9. Cover the pan again and cook for another 5 minutes to allow the flavors to meld together and the paneer to heat through.
10. Once the curry is done, sprinkle garam masala over the curry. Stir gently to combine.

11. Taste and adjust the seasoning if needed.
12. Garnish with fresh coriander leaves before serving.
13. Serve hot with rice, naan, or roti.

Enjoy your homemade Matar Paneer!

Prawn Curry

Ingredients:

- 500g prawns, peeled and deveined
- 2 tablespoons vegetable oil
- 1 onion, finely chopped
- 2 tomatoes, finely chopped or pureed
- 1 tablespoon ginger paste
- 1 tablespoon garlic paste
- 1 green chili, finely chopped (optional)
- 1 teaspoon ground coriander
- 1/2 teaspoon ground cumin
- 1/2 teaspoon turmeric powder
- 1/2 teaspoon red chili powder
- 1/2 teaspoon garam masala
- Salt to taste
- Fresh coriander leaves for garnish

Instructions:

1. Heat vegetable oil in a large pan over medium heat.
2. Add chopped onions and sauté until golden brown.
3. Add ginger paste, garlic paste, and green chili (if using). Sauté for another minute.
4. Add chopped tomatoes (or puree) to the pan. Cook until the tomatoes are soft and oil starts to separate from the mixture, about 5-7 minutes.
5. Add ground coriander, ground cumin, turmeric powder, red chili powder, and salt to the pan. Stir well to combine with the onion-tomato mixture.
6. Add prawns to the pan. Mix well to coat the prawns with the spices.
7. Cover the pan and cook on low heat for about 5-7 minutes, or until the prawns are cooked through and turn pink, stirring occasionally.
8. Once the prawns are cooked, sprinkle garam masala over the curry. Stir gently to combine.
9. Taste and adjust the seasoning if needed.
10. Garnish with fresh coriander leaves before serving.
11. Serve hot with rice, naan, or roti.

Enjoy your homemade Prawn Curry!

Chicken Saag (Chicken with Spinach)

Ingredients:

- 500g chicken pieces (bone-in or boneless)
- 4 cups fresh spinach leaves, washed and chopped
- 2 tablespoons vegetable oil
- 1 onion, finely chopped
- 2 tomatoes, finely chopped or pureed
- 1 tablespoon ginger paste
- 1 tablespoon garlic paste
- 1 green chili, finely chopped (optional)
- 1 teaspoon ground coriander
- 1/2 teaspoon ground cumin
- 1/2 teaspoon turmeric powder
- 1/2 teaspoon red chili powder
- 1/2 teaspoon garam masala
- Salt to taste
- Fresh coriander leaves for garnish

Instructions:

1. Heat vegetable oil in a large pan over medium heat.
2. Add chopped onions and sauté until golden brown.
3. Add ginger paste, garlic paste, and green chili (if using). Sauté for another minute.
4. Add chopped tomatoes (or puree) to the pan. Cook until the tomatoes are soft and oil starts to separate from the mixture, about 5-7 minutes.
5. Add ground coriander, ground cumin, turmeric powder, red chili powder, and salt to the pan. Stir well to combine with the onion-tomato mixture.
6. Add chicken pieces to the pan. Mix well to coat the chicken with the spices.
7. Cover the pan and cook on low heat for about 20-25 minutes, or until the chicken is cooked through, stirring occasionally.
8. Once the chicken is cooked, add chopped spinach leaves to the pan. Stir well to combine with the chicken and spices.
9. Cover the pan again and cook for another 5-7 minutes, or until the spinach wilts down and cooks through.

10. Once the spinach is cooked, sprinkle garam masala over the curry. Stir gently to combine.
11. Taste and adjust the seasoning if needed.
12. Garnish with fresh coriander leaves before serving.
13. Serve hot with rice, naan, or roti.

Enjoy your homemade Chicken Saag!

Dhaba Style Chicken Curry

Ingredients:

- 500g chicken pieces (bone-in or boneless)
- 2 tablespoons vegetable oil
- 2 onions, finely chopped
- 2 tomatoes, finely chopped or pureed
- 1 tablespoon ginger paste
- 1 tablespoon garlic paste
- 2 green chilies, slit lengthwise
- 1 tablespoon yogurt
- 1 teaspoon ground coriander
- 1/2 teaspoon ground cumin
- 1/2 teaspoon turmeric powder
- 1/2 teaspoon red chili powder
- 1/2 teaspoon garam masala
- Salt to taste
- Fresh coriander leaves for garnish

For Tempering:

- 2 tablespoons ghee (clarified butter)
- 1 teaspoon cumin seeds
- 2-3 dried red chilies
- 1 cinnamon stick
- 2-3 green cardamom pods
- 4-5 cloves

Instructions:

1. Heat vegetable oil in a large pan over medium heat.
2. Add chopped onions and sauté until golden brown.
3. Add ginger paste, garlic paste, and green chilies. Sauté for another minute.
4. Add chopped tomatoes (or puree) to the pan. Cook until the tomatoes are soft and oil starts to separate from the mixture, about 5-7 minutes.
5. In a small bowl, whisk yogurt until smooth. Add yogurt to the pan and mix well with the onion-tomato mixture.

6. Add ground coriander, ground cumin, turmeric powder, red chili powder, and salt to the pan. Stir well to combine with the mixture.
7. Add chicken pieces to the pan. Mix well to coat the chicken with the spices.
8. Cover the pan and cook on low heat for about 20-25 minutes, or until the chicken is cooked through, stirring occasionally.
9. In a separate small pan, heat ghee over medium heat for tempering.
10. Add cumin seeds, dried red chilies, cinnamon stick, green cardamom pods, and cloves to the hot ghee. Let them sizzle for a few seconds until fragrant.
11. Pour the tempering over the cooked chicken curry.
12. Sprinkle garam masala over the curry. Stir gently to combine.
13. Taste and adjust the seasoning if needed.
14. Garnish with fresh coriander leaves before serving.
15. Serve hot with rice, naan, or roti.

Enjoy your homemade Dhaba Style Chicken Curry!

Keema Matar (Minced Meat and Peas Curry)

Ingredients:

- 500g minced meat (beef, lamb, or chicken)
- 2 tablespoons vegetable oil
- 1 onion, finely chopped
- 2 tomatoes, finely chopped or pureed
- 1 tablespoon ginger paste
- 1 tablespoon garlic paste
- 1 green chili, finely chopped (optional)
- 1 cup green peas (fresh or frozen)
- 1 teaspoon ground coriander
- 1/2 teaspoon ground cumin
- 1/2 teaspoon turmeric powder
- 1/2 teaspoon red chili powder
- 1/2 teaspoon garam masala
- Salt to taste
- Fresh coriander leaves for garnish

Instructions:

1. Heat vegetable oil in a large pan over medium heat.
2. Add chopped onions and sauté until golden brown.
3. Add ginger paste, garlic paste, and green chili (if using). Sauté for another minute.
4. Add chopped tomatoes (or puree) to the pan. Cook until the tomatoes are soft and oil starts to separate from the mixture, about 5-7 minutes.
5. Add ground coriander, ground cumin, turmeric powder, red chili powder, and salt to the pan. Stir well to combine with the onion-tomato mixture.
6. Add minced meat to the pan. Mix well to coat the meat with the spices.
7. Cook the meat mixture on medium heat until it is browned and cooked through, breaking up any large clumps with a spoon, about 10-15 minutes.
8. Once the meat is cooked, add green peas to the pan. Stir well to combine with the meat mixture.
9. Cover the pan and simmer on low heat for about 5-7 minutes, or until the peas are cooked through, stirring occasionally.

10. Once the peas are cooked, sprinkle garam masala over the curry. Stir gently to combine.
11. Taste and adjust the seasoning if needed.
12. Garnish with fresh coriander leaves before serving.
13. Serve hot with rice, naan, or roti.

Enjoy your homemade Keema Matar!

Dum Aloo (Potatoes in Spicy Gravy)

Ingredients:

- 500g baby potatoes, boiled and peeled
- 2 tablespoons vegetable oil
- 1 onion, finely chopped
- 2 tomatoes, finely chopped or pureed
- 1 tablespoon ginger paste
- 1 tablespoon garlic paste
- 1 green chili, finely chopped (optional)
- 1 teaspoon ground coriander
- 1/2 teaspoon ground cumin
- 1/2 teaspoon turmeric powder
- 1/2 teaspoon red chili powder
- 1/2 teaspoon garam masala
- Salt to taste
- Fresh coriander leaves for garnish

For the Marinade:

- 1 cup yogurt
- 1 teaspoon Kashmiri red chili powder (for color)
- 1/2 teaspoon turmeric powder
- Salt to taste

Instructions:

1. In a bowl, mix together yogurt, Kashmiri red chili powder, turmeric powder, and salt to prepare the marinade.
2. Prick the boiled baby potatoes with a fork and marinate them in the prepared yogurt mixture. Allow them to marinate for at least 30 minutes.
3. Heat vegetable oil in a large pan over medium heat.
4. Add chopped onions and sauté until golden brown.
5. Add ginger paste, garlic paste, and green chili (if using). Sauté for another minute.
6. Add chopped tomatoes (or puree) to the pan. Cook until the tomatoes are soft and oil starts to separate from the mixture, about 5-7 minutes.

7. Add ground coriander, ground cumin, turmeric powder, red chili powder, and salt to the pan. Stir well to combine with the onion-tomato mixture.
8. Add marinated potatoes along with the marinade to the pan. Mix well to coat the potatoes with the spices.
9. Cover the pan and simmer on low heat for about 15-20 minutes, allowing the potatoes to absorb the flavors of the spices and yogurt, stirring occasionally.
10. Once the potatoes are cooked through and the gravy has thickened, sprinkle garam masala over the curry. Stir gently to combine.
11. Taste and adjust the seasoning if needed.
12. Garnish with fresh coriander leaves before serving.
13. Serve hot with rice, naan, or roti.

Enjoy your homemade Dum Aloo!

Fish Tikka Masala

Ingredients:

For the Fish Marinade:

- 500g firm white fish fillets (such as tilapia or cod), cut into bite-sized pieces
- 1 cup plain yogurt
- 1 tablespoon ginger paste
- 1 tablespoon garlic paste
- 1 tablespoon lemon juice
- 1 teaspoon ground cumin
- 1 teaspoon ground coriander
- 1/2 teaspoon turmeric powder
- 1/2 teaspoon Kashmiri red chili powder (for color)
- 1/2 teaspoon garam masala
- Salt to taste

For the Tikka Masala Sauce:

- 2 tablespoons vegetable oil
- 1 onion, finely chopped
- 2 tomatoes, finely chopped or pureed
- 1 tablespoon ginger paste
- 1 tablespoon garlic paste
- 1 green chili, finely chopped (optional)
- 1 teaspoon ground coriander
- 1/2 teaspoon ground cumin
- 1/2 teaspoon turmeric powder
- 1/2 teaspoon red chili powder
- 1/2 teaspoon garam masala
- 1/2 cup heavy cream
- Salt to taste
- Fresh coriander leaves for garnish

Instructions:

1. In a bowl, mix together all the ingredients for the fish marinade until well combined.

2. Add the fish pieces to the marinade, ensuring they are well coated. Cover and refrigerate for at least 30 minutes, or ideally, marinate overnight for maximum flavor.
3. Preheat the oven to 200°C (400°F). Thread the marinated fish pieces onto skewers and place them on a baking tray lined with aluminum foil. Bake for 15-20 minutes or until the fish is cooked through and lightly browned.
4. While the fish is baking, prepare the tikka masala sauce. Heat vegetable oil in a large pan over medium heat.
5. Add chopped onions and sauté until golden brown.
6. Add ginger paste, garlic paste, and green chili (if using). Sauté for another minute.
7. Add chopped tomatoes (or puree) to the pan. Cook until the tomatoes are soft and oil starts to separate from the mixture, about 5-7 minutes.
8. Add ground coriander, ground cumin, turmeric powder, red chili powder, and salt to the pan. Stir well to combine with the onion-tomato mixture.
9. Cook the spices for 2-3 minutes until fragrant.
10. Add heavy cream to the pan and mix well. Allow the sauce to simmer for 5-7 minutes until it thickens slightly.
11. Once the fish is cooked, carefully remove the skewers from the oven and add the fish pieces to the simmering sauce.
12. Sprinkle garam masala over the curry. Stir gently to combine.
13. Taste and adjust the seasoning if needed.
14. Garnish with fresh coriander leaves before serving.
15. Serve hot with rice or naan.

Enjoy your homemade Fish Tikka Masala!

Tofu Tikka Masala

Ingredients:

For the Tofu Marinade:

- 400g firm tofu, drained and pressed, cut into cubes
- 1 cup plain yogurt
- 1 tablespoon ginger paste
- 1 tablespoon garlic paste
- 1 tablespoon lemon juice
- 1 teaspoon ground cumin
- 1 teaspoon ground coriander
- 1/2 teaspoon turmeric powder
- 1/2 teaspoon Kashmiri red chili powder (for color)
- 1/2 teaspoon garam masala
- Salt to taste

For the Tikka Masala Sauce:

- 2 tablespoons vegetable oil
- 1 onion, finely chopped
- 2 tomatoes, finely chopped or pureed
- 1 tablespoon ginger paste
- 1 tablespoon garlic paste
- 1 green chili, finely chopped (optional)
- 1 teaspoon ground coriander
- 1/2 teaspoon ground cumin
- 1/2 teaspoon turmeric powder
- 1/2 teaspoon red chili powder
- 1/2 teaspoon garam masala
- 1/2 cup coconut milk
- Salt to taste
- Fresh coriander leaves for garnish

Instructions:

1. In a bowl, mix together all the ingredients for the tofu marinade until well combined.

2. Add the tofu cubes to the marinade, ensuring they are well coated. Cover and refrigerate for at least 30 minutes to allow the flavors to meld.
3. Preheat the oven to 200°C (400°F). Thread the marinated tofu cubes onto skewers and place them on a baking tray lined with aluminum foil. Bake for 20-25 minutes or until the tofu is golden brown and slightly crispy.
4. While the tofu is baking, prepare the tikka masala sauce. Heat vegetable oil in a large pan over medium heat.
5. Add chopped onions and sauté until golden brown.
6. Add ginger paste, garlic paste, and green chili (if using). Sauté for another minute.
7. Add chopped tomatoes (or puree) to the pan. Cook until the tomatoes are soft and oil starts to separate from the mixture, about 5-7 minutes.
8. Add ground coriander, ground cumin, turmeric powder, red chili powder, and salt to the pan. Stir well to combine with the onion-tomato mixture.
9. Cook the spices for 2-3 minutes until fragrant.
10. Add coconut milk to the pan and mix well. Allow the sauce to simmer for 5-7 minutes until it thickens slightly.
11. Once the tofu is cooked, carefully remove the skewers from the oven and add the tofu cubes to the simmering sauce.
12. Sprinkle garam masala over the curry. Stir gently to combine.
13. Taste and adjust the seasoning if needed.
14. Garnish with fresh coriander leaves before serving.
15. Serve hot with rice or naan.

Enjoy your homemade Tofu Tikka Masala!

Vegetable Korma

Ingredients:

- 2 cups mixed vegetables (such as carrots, peas, cauliflower, potatoes), chopped
- 1 onion, finely chopped
- 2 tomatoes, finely chopped or pureed
- 1/2 cup unsweetened coconut milk
- 1/4 cup plain yogurt
- 2 tablespoons vegetable oil
- 1 teaspoon ginger paste
- 1 teaspoon garlic paste
- 1 green chili, finely chopped (optional)
- 1 teaspoon ground coriander
- 1/2 teaspoon ground cumin
- 1/2 teaspoon turmeric powder
- 1/2 teaspoon red chili powder
- 1/2 teaspoon garam masala
- Salt to taste
- Fresh coriander leaves for garnish

For the Korma Paste:

- 1/2 cup unsweetened shredded coconut
- 2 tablespoons cashew nuts or almonds
- 1 tablespoon poppy seeds (optional)
- 1 tablespoon fennel seeds
- 1 tablespoon coriander seeds
- 2-3 green cardamom pods
- 2-3 cloves
- 1-inch cinnamon stick

Instructions:

1. Heat a dry skillet over medium heat. Add all the ingredients for the korma paste (shredded coconut, cashew nuts or almonds, poppy seeds, fennel seeds, coriander seeds, cardamom pods, cloves, and cinnamon stick). Toast the spices and nuts until fragrant and lightly browned, about 3-5 minutes. Remove from heat and let it cool.

2. Once cooled, transfer the toasted ingredients to a blender or food processor. Add a little water and blend into a smooth paste. Set aside.
3. Heat vegetable oil in a large pan over medium heat. Add chopped onions and sauté until golden brown.
4. Add ginger paste, garlic paste, and green chili (if using). Sauté for another minute.
5. Add chopped tomatoes (or puree) to the pan. Cook until the tomatoes are soft and oil starts to separate from the mixture, about 5-7 minutes.
6. Add the korma paste to the pan. Stir well to combine with the onion-tomato mixture.
7. Add ground coriander, ground cumin, turmeric powder, red chili powder, and salt to the pan. Mix well.
8. Add mixed vegetables to the pan. Stir to coat the vegetables with the spice mixture.
9. Add unsweetened coconut milk and plain yogurt to the pan. Mix well to combine.
10. Cover the pan and simmer on low heat for about 15-20 minutes, or until the vegetables are cooked through and the sauce thickens, stirring occasionally.
11. Once the vegetables are cooked, sprinkle garam masala over the korma. Stir gently to combine.
12. Taste and adjust the seasoning if needed.
13. Garnish with fresh coriander leaves before serving.
14. Serve hot with rice, naan, or roti.

Enjoy your homemade Vegetable Korma!

Egg Masala

Ingredients:

- 6 hard-boiled eggs, peeled and halved
- 2 tablespoons vegetable oil
- 1 onion, finely chopped
- 2 tomatoes, finely chopped or pureed
- 1 tablespoon ginger paste
- 1 tablespoon garlic paste
- 1 green chili, finely chopped (optional)
- 1 teaspoon ground coriander
- 1/2 teaspoon ground cumin
- 1/2 teaspoon turmeric powder
- 1/2 teaspoon red chili powder
- 1/2 teaspoon garam masala
- Salt to taste
- Fresh coriander leaves for garnish

Instructions:

1. Heat vegetable oil in a large pan over medium heat.
2. Add chopped onions and sauté until golden brown.
3. Add ginger paste, garlic paste, and green chili (if using). Sauté for another minute.
4. Add chopped tomatoes (or puree) to the pan. Cook until the tomatoes are soft and oil starts to separate from the mixture, about 5-7 minutes.
5. Add ground coriander, ground cumin, turmeric powder, red chili powder, and salt to the pan. Stir well to combine with the onion-tomato mixture.
6. Add the halved hard-boiled eggs to the pan. Gently mix with the spice mixture, ensuring the eggs are coated evenly.
7. Cover the pan and simmer on low heat for about 5-7 minutes, allowing the eggs to absorb the flavors of the spices, stirring occasionally.
8. Once the eggs are heated through and the sauce has thickened slightly, sprinkle garam masala over the curry. Stir gently to combine.
9. Taste and adjust the seasoning if needed.
10. Garnish with fresh coriander leaves before serving.
11. Serve hot with rice, naan, or roti.

Enjoy your homemade Egg Masala!

Chicken Vindaloo

Ingredients:

- 500g chicken pieces (bone-in or boneless)
- 2 tablespoons vegetable oil
- 2 onions, finely chopped
- 4 cloves garlic, minced
- 1-inch ginger, minced
- 2 tomatoes, finely chopped or pureed
- 2 tablespoons malt vinegar or apple cider vinegar
- 1 tablespoon tomato paste
- 1 teaspoon sugar
- 1 teaspoon mustard seeds
- 1 teaspoon cumin seeds
- 1 teaspoon ground turmeric
- 2 teaspoons ground coriander
- 1 teaspoon paprika
- 1/2 teaspoon ground cinnamon
- 1/2 teaspoon ground cloves
- 1/2 teaspoon cayenne pepper (adjust to taste)
- Salt to taste
- Fresh coriander leaves for garnish

Instructions:

1. Heat vegetable oil in a large pan over medium heat. Add mustard seeds and cumin seeds. Let them splutter.
2. Add chopped onions and sauté until they turn golden brown.
3. Add minced garlic and ginger. Sauté for another minute until fragrant.
4. Add chopped tomatoes (or puree) to the pan. Cook until the tomatoes are soft and oil starts to separate from the mixture, about 5-7 minutes.
5. Stir in tomato paste, malt vinegar (or apple cider vinegar), sugar, ground turmeric, ground coriander, paprika, ground cinnamon, ground cloves, cayenne pepper, and salt. Mix well.
6. Add chicken pieces to the pan. Mix well to coat the chicken with the spice mixture.

7. Cover the pan and cook on low heat for about 20-25 minutes, or until the chicken is cooked through, stirring occasionally.
8. Once the chicken is cooked, taste and adjust the seasoning if needed.
9. Garnish with fresh coriander leaves before serving.
10. Serve hot with rice, naan, or roti.

Enjoy your homemade Chicken Vindaloo! Adjust the amount of cayenne pepper according to your spice preference.

Lauki Kofta (Bottle Gourd Dumplings in Gravy)

Ingredients:

For the Koftas (Dumplings):

- 2 cups grated bottle gourd (lauki)
- 1/2 cup besan (gram flour)
- 1 green chili, finely chopped
- 1 tablespoon ginger paste
- 1 tablespoon garlic paste
- 1/2 teaspoon ground cumin
- 1/2 teaspoon ground coriander
- 1/2 teaspoon red chili powder
- 1/4 teaspoon turmeric powder
- Salt to taste
- Vegetable oil for frying

For the Gravy:

- 2 tablespoons vegetable oil
- 1 onion, finely chopped
- 2 tomatoes, finely chopped or pureed
- 1 tablespoon ginger paste
- 1 tablespoon garlic paste
- 1 green chili, finely chopped
- 1 teaspoon ground coriander
- 1/2 teaspoon ground cumin
- 1/2 teaspoon turmeric powder
- 1/2 teaspoon red chili powder
- 1/2 teaspoon garam masala
- Salt to taste
- Fresh coriander leaves for garnish

Instructions:

1. To make the koftas, squeeze out excess water from the grated bottle gourd using your hands or a cheesecloth. Transfer the grated bottle gourd to a mixing bowl.

2. Add besan, green chili, ginger paste, garlic paste, ground cumin, ground coriander, red chili powder, turmeric powder, and salt to the grated bottle gourd. Mix well to form a dough-like mixture.
3. Heat vegetable oil in a deep frying pan over medium heat.
4. Take small portions of the mixture and shape them into round balls to form koftas.
5. Carefully drop the koftas into the hot oil and fry until they turn golden brown and crispy on all sides. Remove them from the oil and drain excess oil on paper towels. Set aside.
6. To make the gravy, heat vegetable oil in a large pan over medium heat.
7. Add chopped onions and sauté until golden brown.
8. Add ginger paste, garlic paste, and green chili. Sauté for another minute until fragrant.
9. Add chopped tomatoes (or puree) to the pan. Cook until the tomatoes are soft and oil starts to separate from the mixture, about 5-7 minutes.
10. Add ground coriander, ground cumin, turmeric powder, red chili powder, and salt to the pan. Stir well to combine with the onion-tomato mixture.
11. Add water to adjust the consistency of the gravy. Bring the gravy to a gentle boil.
12. Add the fried koftas to the gravy. Simmer on low heat for about 10-15 minutes to allow the koftas to absorb the flavors of the gravy.
13. Once the koftas are heated through and the gravy has thickened, sprinkle garam masala over the curry. Stir gently to combine.
14. Taste and adjust the seasoning if needed.
15. Garnish with fresh coriander leaves before serving.
16. Serve hot with rice, naan, or roti.

Enjoy your homemade Lauki Kofta!

Baingan Ka Salan (Eggplant Curry in Peanut Sauce)

Ingredients:

- 2 large eggplants (baingan), cut into cubes
- 2 tablespoons vegetable oil
- 1 onion, finely chopped
- 2 tomatoes, finely chopped or pureed
- 1 tablespoon tamarind paste
- 1 tablespoon jaggery or sugar
- 1/4 cup roasted peanuts, ground into a paste
- 1 teaspoon mustard seeds
- 1 teaspoon cumin seeds
- 1/2 teaspoon fenugreek seeds
- 1/2 teaspoon turmeric powder
- 1/2 teaspoon red chili powder
- Salt to taste
- Fresh coriander leaves for garnish

Instructions:

1. Heat vegetable oil in a large pan over medium heat.
2. Add mustard seeds, cumin seeds, and fenugreek seeds. Let them splutter.
3. Add chopped onions and sauté until golden brown.
4. Add chopped tomatoes (or puree) to the pan. Cook until the tomatoes are soft and oil starts to separate from the mixture, about 5-7 minutes.
5. Add tamarind paste, jaggery (or sugar), ground peanuts, turmeric powder, red chili powder, and salt to the pan. Mix well.
6. Add cubed eggplants to the pan. Stir gently to coat the eggplants with the sauce.
7. Cover the pan and cook on low heat for about 15-20 minutes, or until the eggplants are tender, stirring occasionally.
8. Once the eggplants are cooked through, taste and adjust the seasoning if needed.
9. Garnish with fresh coriander leaves before serving.
10. Serve hot with rice or roti.

Enjoy your homemade Baingan Ka Salan! Adjust the amount of red chili powder according to your spice preference.

Methi Malai Paneer (Paneer in Fenugreek Cream Sauce)

Ingredients:

- 200g paneer, cut into cubes
- 2 tablespoons ghee or butter
- 1 onion, finely chopped
- 2 tomatoes, finely chopped or pureed
- 1 tablespoon ginger paste
- 1 tablespoon garlic paste
- 1 green chili, finely chopped (optional)
- 1 cup fresh fenugreek leaves (methi), washed and finely chopped
- 1/2 cup heavy cream
- 1/4 cup milk
- 1/2 teaspoon garam masala
- 1/2 teaspoon ground coriander
- 1/4 teaspoon ground turmeric
- 1/4 teaspoon red chili powder
- Salt to taste
- Fresh coriander leaves for garnish

Instructions:

1. Heat ghee or butter in a large pan over medium heat.
2. Add chopped onions and sauté until golden brown.
3. Add ginger paste, garlic paste, and green chili (if using). Sauté for another minute.
4. Add chopped tomatoes (or puree) to the pan. Cook until the tomatoes are soft and oil starts to separate from the mixture, about 5-7 minutes.
5. Add ground coriander, ground turmeric, red chili powder, and salt to the pan. Stir well to combine with the onion-tomato mixture.
6. Add chopped fenugreek leaves (methi) to the pan. Cook for 2-3 minutes until the leaves wilt down.
7. Lower the heat and add heavy cream and milk to the pan. Mix well to combine.
8. Allow the mixture to simmer for 5-7 minutes, stirring occasionally.
9. Add paneer cubes to the pan. Gently mix with the sauce, ensuring the paneer is coated evenly.

10. Cover the pan and cook on low heat for another 5 minutes to allow the flavors to meld together.
11. Sprinkle garam masala over the dish. Stir gently to combine.
12. Taste and adjust the seasoning if needed.
13. Garnish with fresh coriander leaves before serving.
14. Serve hot with rice, naan, or roti.

Enjoy your homemade Methi Malai Paneer! Adjust the amount of green chili and red chili powder according to your spice preference.

Chicken Do Pyaza (Chicken Curry with Double Onions)

Ingredients:

- 500g chicken pieces (bone-in or boneless)
- 2 large onions, thinly sliced
- 2 tomatoes, finely chopped or pureed
- 2 tablespoons vegetable oil
- 1 tablespoon ginger paste
- 1 tablespoon garlic paste
- 1 green chili, finely chopped
- 1 teaspoon ground coriander
- 1/2 teaspoon ground cumin
- 1/2 teaspoon turmeric powder
- 1/2 teaspoon red chili powder
- 1/2 teaspoon garam masala
- Salt to taste
- Fresh coriander leaves for garnish

Instructions:

1. Heat vegetable oil in a large pan over medium heat.
2. Add thinly sliced onions and sauté until they turn golden brown and caramelized.
3. Remove half of the caramelized onions from the pan and set aside for later use.
4. To the remaining onions in the pan, add ginger paste, garlic paste, and green chili. Sauté for another minute until fragrant.
5. Add chopped tomatoes (or puree) to the pan. Cook until the tomatoes are soft and oil starts to separate from the mixture, about 5-7 minutes.
6. Add ground coriander, ground cumin, turmeric powder, red chili powder, and salt to the pan. Stir well to combine with the onion-tomato mixture.
7. Add chicken pieces to the pan. Mix well to coat the chicken with the spice mixture.
8. Cover the pan and cook on low heat for about 20-25 minutes, or until the chicken is cooked through, stirring occasionally.
9. Once the chicken is cooked, add the reserved caramelized onions back to the pan. Mix well.
10. Sprinkle garam masala over the curry. Stir gently to combine.
11. Taste and adjust the seasoning if needed.

12. Garnish with fresh coriander leaves before serving.
13. Serve hot with rice, naan, or roti.

Enjoy your homemade Chicken Do Pyaza! Adjust the amount of green chili and red chili powder according to your spice preference.

Achari Chicken (Pickled Spice Chicken Curry)

Ingredients:

- 500g chicken pieces (bone-in or boneless)
- 2 tablespoons vegetable oil
- 2 onions, finely chopped
- 2 tomatoes, finely chopped or pureed
- 1 tablespoon ginger paste
- 1 tablespoon garlic paste
- 2 green chilies, slit lengthwise
- 1 tablespoon mustard seeds
- 1 tablespoon fenugreek seeds
- 1 tablespoon fennel seeds
- 1 tablespoon cumin seeds
- 1 tablespoon coriander seeds
- 1/2 teaspoon nigella seeds (kalonji)
- 1/2 teaspoon fenugreek powder
- 1/2 teaspoon turmeric powder
- 1/2 teaspoon red chili powder
- Salt to taste
- Fresh coriander leaves for garnish

Instructions:

1. Heat vegetable oil in a large pan over medium heat.
2. Add mustard seeds, fenugreek seeds, fennel seeds, cumin seeds, coriander seeds, and nigella seeds (kalonji). Let them splutter.
3. Add chopped onions and sauté until golden brown.
4. Add ginger paste, garlic paste, and green chilies. Sauté for another minute.
5. Add chopped tomatoes (or puree) to the pan. Cook until the tomatoes are soft and oil starts to separate from the mixture, about 5-7 minutes.
6. Add ground fenugreek powder, turmeric powder, red chili powder, and salt to the pan. Stir well to combine with the onion-tomato mixture.
7. Add chicken pieces to the pan. Mix well to coat the chicken with the spice mixture.
8. Cover the pan and cook on low heat for about 20-25 minutes, or until the chicken is cooked through, stirring occasionally.
9. Once the chicken is cooked, taste and adjust the seasoning if needed.

10. Garnish with fresh coriander leaves before serving.
11. Serve hot with rice, naan, or roti.

Enjoy your homemade Achari Chicken! Adjust the amount of green chilies and red chili powder according to your spice preference.

Dum Paneer Kali Mirch (Paneer in Black Pepper Sauce)

Ingredients:

- 200g paneer, cut into cubes
- 2 tablespoons ghee or butter
- 1 onion, finely chopped
- 2 tomatoes, finely chopped or pureed
- 1 tablespoon ginger paste
- 1 tablespoon garlic paste
- 1 green chili, finely chopped
- 1 tablespoon black peppercorns, crushed
- 1/2 teaspoon turmeric powder
- 1/2 teaspoon ground cumin
- 1/2 teaspoon garam masala
- 1/2 cup heavy cream
- Salt to taste
- Fresh coriander leaves for garnish

Instructions:

1. Heat ghee or butter in a large pan over medium heat.
2. Add chopped onions and sauté until golden brown.
3. Add ginger paste, garlic paste, and green chili. Sauté for another minute until fragrant.
4. Add chopped tomatoes (or puree) to the pan. Cook until the tomatoes are soft and oil starts to separate from the mixture, about 5-7 minutes.
5. Add crushed black peppercorns, turmeric powder, ground cumin, and salt to the pan. Stir well to combine with the onion-tomato mixture.
6. Add paneer cubes to the pan. Mix gently with the sauce, ensuring the paneer is coated evenly.
7. Cover the pan and cook on low heat for about 5 minutes, allowing the flavors to meld together.
8. Add heavy cream to the pan. Mix well and simmer for another 2-3 minutes.
9. Sprinkle garam masala over the dish. Stir gently to combine.
10. Taste and adjust the seasoning if needed.
11. Garnish with fresh coriander leaves before serving.
12. Serve hot with rice, naan, or roti.

Enjoy your homemade Dum Paneer Kali Mirch! Adjust the amount of black peppercorns and green chili according to your spice preference.

Mutton Curry

Ingredients:

- 500g mutton pieces (bone-in preferred)
- 3 tablespoons vegetable oil
- 2 onions, finely chopped
- 2 tomatoes, finely chopped or pureed
- 1 tablespoon ginger paste
- 1 tablespoon garlic paste
- 2 green chilies, slit lengthwise
- 1 teaspoon ground coriander
- 1/2 teaspoon ground cumin
- 1/2 teaspoon turmeric powder
- 1/2 teaspoon red chili powder
- 1/2 teaspoon garam masala
- Salt to taste
- Fresh coriander leaves for garnish

Instructions:

1. Heat vegetable oil in a pressure cooker or large pot over medium heat.
2. Add chopped onions and sauté until golden brown.
3. Add ginger paste, garlic paste, and green chilies. Sauté for another minute until fragrant.
4. Add chopped tomatoes (or puree) to the pot. Cook until the tomatoes are soft and oil starts to separate from the mixture, about 5-7 minutes.
5. Add ground coriander, ground cumin, turmeric powder, red chili powder, and salt to the pot. Stir well to combine with the onion-tomato mixture.
6. Add mutton pieces to the pot. Mix well to coat the mutton with the spice mixture.
7. If using a pressure cooker, add about 1 cup of water. Close the lid and pressure cook for about 4-5 whistles, or until the mutton is tender.
8. If using a regular pot, add enough water to cover the mutton pieces. Cover the pot and simmer on low heat for about 1.5 to 2 hours, or until the mutton is tender, stirring occasionally and adding more water if needed.
9. Once the mutton is cooked and tender, sprinkle garam masala over the curry. Stir gently to combine.
10. Taste and adjust the seasoning if needed.

11. Garnish with fresh coriander leaves before serving.
12. Serve hot with rice, naan, or roti.

Enjoy your homemade Mutton Curry! Adjust the amount of green chilies and red chili powder according to your spice preference.

Coconut Chicken Curry

Ingredients:

- 500g chicken pieces (bone-in or boneless)
- 2 tablespoons vegetable oil
- 1 onion, finely chopped
- 2 tomatoes, finely chopped or pureed
- 1 tablespoon ginger paste
- 1 tablespoon garlic paste
- 2 green chilies, slit lengthwise
- 1 cup coconut milk
- 1/2 cup water
- 1 teaspoon ground coriander
- 1/2 teaspoon ground cumin
- 1/2 teaspoon turmeric powder
- 1/2 teaspoon red chili powder
- 1/2 teaspoon garam masala
- Salt to taste
- Fresh coriander leaves for garnish

Instructions:

1. Heat vegetable oil in a large pan over medium heat.
2. Add chopped onions and sauté until golden brown.
3. Add ginger paste, garlic paste, and green chilies. Sauté for another minute until fragrant.
4. Add chopped tomatoes (or puree) to the pan. Cook until the tomatoes are soft and oil starts to separate from the mixture, about 5-7 minutes.
5. Add ground coriander, ground cumin, turmeric powder, red chili powder, and salt to the pan. Stir well to combine with the onion-tomato mixture.
6. Add chicken pieces to the pan. Mix well to coat the chicken with the spice mixture.
7. Add coconut milk and water to the pan. Mix well.
8. Cover the pan and simmer on low heat for about 20-25 minutes, or until the chicken is cooked through, stirring occasionally.
9. Once the chicken is cooked, sprinkle garam masala over the curry. Stir gently to combine.

10. Taste and adjust the seasoning if needed.
11. Garnish with fresh coriander leaves before serving.
12. Serve hot with rice, naan, or roti.

Enjoy your homemade Coconut Chicken Curry! Adjust the amount of green chilies and red chili powder according to your spice preference.

Jackfruit Curry (Kathal Ki Sabzi)

Ingredients:

- 500g raw jackfruit (kathal), cut into bite-sized pieces
- 2 tablespoons vegetable oil
- 1 onion, finely chopped
- 2 tomatoes, finely chopped or pureed
- 1 tablespoon ginger paste
- 1 tablespoon garlic paste
- 2 green chilies, slit lengthwise
- 1 teaspoon cumin seeds
- 1 teaspoon ground coriander
- 1/2 teaspoon ground turmeric
- 1/2 teaspoon red chili powder
- 1/2 teaspoon garam masala
- Salt to taste
- Fresh coriander leaves for garnish

Instructions:

1. Heat vegetable oil in a large pan over medium heat.
2. Add cumin seeds and let them splutter.
3. Add chopped onions and sauté until golden brown.
4. Add ginger paste, garlic paste, and green chilies. Sauté for another minute until fragrant.
5. Add chopped tomatoes (or puree) to the pan. Cook until the tomatoes are soft and oil starts to separate from the mixture, about 5-7 minutes.
6. Add ground coriander, ground turmeric, red chili powder, and salt to the pan. Stir well to combine with the onion-tomato mixture.
7. Add jackfruit pieces to the pan. Mix well to coat the jackfruit with the spice mixture.
8. Add a little water if needed to prevent the mixture from sticking to the pan. Cover and cook on low heat for about 20-25 minutes, or until the jackfruit is tender, stirring occasionally.
9. Once the jackfruit is cooked, sprinkle garam masala over the curry. Stir gently to combine.
10. Taste and adjust the seasoning if needed.
11. Garnish with fresh coriander leaves before serving.

12. Serve hot with rice, roti, or naan.

Enjoy your homemade Jackfruit Curry (Kathal Ki Sabzi)! Adjust the amount of green chilies and red chili powder according to your spice preference.

Bhuna Chicken (Dry Chicken Curry)

Ingredients:

- 500g chicken pieces (bone-in or boneless)
- 2 tablespoons vegetable oil
- 2 onions, finely chopped
- 2 tomatoes, finely chopped or pureed
- 1 tablespoon ginger paste
- 1 tablespoon garlic paste
- 2 green chilies, slit lengthwise
- 1 teaspoon cumin seeds
- 1 teaspoon coriander seeds, crushed
- 1/2 teaspoon turmeric powder
- 1/2 teaspoon red chili powder
- 1/2 teaspoon garam masala
- Salt to taste
- Fresh coriander leaves for garnish

Instructions:

1. Heat vegetable oil in a large pan over medium heat.
2. Add cumin seeds and crushed coriander seeds. Let them splutter.
3. Add chopped onions and sauté until golden brown.
4. Add ginger paste, garlic paste, and green chilies. Sauté for another minute until fragrant.
5. Add chopped tomatoes (or puree) to the pan. Cook until the tomatoes are soft and oil starts to separate from the mixture, about 5-7 minutes.
6. Add ground turmeric, red chili powder, and salt to the pan. Stir well to combine with the onion-tomato mixture.
7. Add chicken pieces to the pan. Mix well to coat the chicken with the spice mixture.
8. Cover the pan and cook on low heat for about 20-25 minutes, or until the chicken is cooked through, stirring occasionally.
9. Once the chicken is cooked, sprinkle garam masala over the curry. Stir gently to combine.

10. Increase the heat to medium-high and cook for another 5-7 minutes, stirring continuously, until the excess moisture evaporates and the curry thickens. This step is essential to achieve the "bhuna" texture.
11. Taste and adjust the seasoning if needed.
12. Garnish with fresh coriander leaves before serving.
13. Serve hot with rice, roti, or naan.

Enjoy your homemade Bhuna Chicken! Adjust the amount of green chilies and red chili powder according to your spice preference.

Shahi Paneer (Royal Paneer Curry)

Ingredients:

- 200g paneer, cut into cubes
- 2 tablespoons ghee or butter
- 1 onion, finely chopped
- 2 tomatoes, finely chopped or pureed
- 1 tablespoon ginger paste
- 1 tablespoon garlic paste
- 2 green chilies, slit lengthwise
- 1/4 cup cashew nuts, soaked in warm water for 30 minutes
- 1/4 cup milk
- 1/4 cup cream
- 1/2 teaspoon turmeric powder
- 1/2 teaspoon ground coriander
- 1/2 teaspoon red chili powder
- 1/2 teaspoon garam masala
- Salt to taste
- Fresh coriander leaves for garnish

Instructions:

1. Heat ghee or butter in a large pan over medium heat.
2. Add chopped onions and sauté until golden brown.
3. Add ginger paste, garlic paste, and green chilies. Sauté for another minute until fragrant.
4. Add chopped tomatoes (or puree) to the pan. Cook until the tomatoes are soft and oil starts to separate from the mixture, about 5-7 minutes.
5. Drain the soaked cashew nuts and transfer them to a blender or food processor. Add milk and blend into a smooth paste.
6. Add the cashew paste to the pan. Mix well with the onion-tomato mixture.
7. Add ground turmeric, ground coriander, red chili powder, and salt to the pan. Stir well to combine.
8. Add paneer cubes to the pan. Mix gently to coat the paneer with the sauce.
9. Cover the pan and simmer on low heat for about 5 minutes, allowing the flavors to meld together.
10. Add cream to the pan. Mix well and simmer for another 2-3 minutes.

11. Sprinkle garam masala over the dish. Stir gently to combine.
12. Taste and adjust the seasoning if needed.
13. Garnish with fresh coriander leaves before serving.
14. Serve hot with rice, naan, or roti.

Enjoy your homemade Shahi Paneer! Adjust the amount of green chilies and red chili powder according to your spice preference.

Amritsari Chole (Punjabi Style Chickpea Curry)

Ingredients:

- 2 cups dried chickpeas (chole), soaked overnight and drained
- 2 tablespoons vegetable oil
- 2 onions, finely chopped
- 2 tomatoes, finely chopped or pureed
- 1 tablespoon ginger paste
- 1 tablespoon garlic paste
- 2 green chilies, slit lengthwise
- 1 teaspoon cumin seeds
- 2 teaspoons Amchur (dried mango powder)
- 1 teaspoon ground coriander
- 1/2 teaspoon ground cumin
- 1/2 teaspoon turmeric powder
- 1/2 teaspoon red chili powder
- 1/2 teaspoon garam masala
- Salt to taste
- Fresh coriander leaves for garnish

Instructions:

1. Heat vegetable oil in a pressure cooker or large pot over medium heat.
2. Add cumin seeds and let them splutter.
3. Add chopped onions and sauté until golden brown.
4. Add ginger paste, garlic paste, and green chilies. Sauté for another minute until fragrant.
5. Add chopped tomatoes (or puree) to the pot. Cook until the tomatoes are soft and oil starts to separate from the mixture, about 5-7 minutes.
6. Add ground coriander, ground cumin, turmeric powder, red chili powder, Amchur, and salt to the pot. Stir well to combine.
7. Add soaked chickpeas to the pot. Mix well to coat the chickpeas with the spice mixture.
8. If using a pressure cooker, add about 3 cups of water. Close the lid and pressure cook for about 4-5 whistles, or until the chickpeas are tender.

9. If using a regular pot, add enough water to cover the chickpeas. Cover the pot and simmer on low heat for about 1.5 to 2 hours, or until the chickpeas are tender, stirring occasionally and adding more water if needed.
10. Once the chickpeas are cooked, sprinkle garam masala over the curry. Stir gently to combine.
11. Taste and adjust the seasoning if needed.
12. Garnish with fresh coriander leaves before serving.
13. Serve hot with rice, naan, or roti.

Enjoy your homemade Amritsari Chole! Adjust the amount of green chilies and red chili powder according to your spice preference.

Kadai Paneer (Paneer and Bell Pepper Curry)

Ingredients:

- 200g paneer, cut into cubes
- 1 large bell pepper (capsicum), cut into strips
- 2 tablespoons vegetable oil
- 1 onion, finely chopped
- 2 tomatoes, finely chopped or pureed
- 1 tablespoon ginger paste
- 1 tablespoon garlic paste
- 2 green chilies, slit lengthwise
- 1 teaspoon cumin seeds
- 1 teaspoon coriander seeds, crushed
- 1 teaspoon kasuri methi (dried fenugreek leaves)
- 1/2 teaspoon turmeric powder
- 1/2 teaspoon red chili powder
- 1/2 teaspoon garam masala
- Salt to taste
- Fresh coriander leaves for garnish

Instructions:

1. Heat vegetable oil in a large pan or kadai over medium heat.
2. Add cumin seeds and let them splutter.
3. Add chopped onions and sauté until golden brown.
4. Add ginger paste, garlic paste, and green chilies. Sauté for another minute until fragrant.
5. Add chopped tomatoes (or puree) to the pan. Cook until the tomatoes are soft and oil starts to separate from the mixture, about 5-7 minutes.
6. Add crushed coriander seeds, kasuri methi, turmeric powder, red chili powder, and salt to the pan. Stir well to combine.
7. Add bell pepper strips to the pan. Mix well with the onion-tomato mixture and cook for 3-4 minutes.
8. Add paneer cubes to the pan. Gently mix with the sauce, ensuring the paneer is coated evenly.
9. Cover the pan and cook on low heat for about 5 minutes, allowing the flavors to meld together.

10. Sprinkle garam masala over the dish. Stir gently to combine.
11. Taste and adjust the seasoning if needed.
12. Garnish with fresh coriander leaves before serving.
13. Serve hot with rice, naan, or roti.

Enjoy your homemade Kadai Paneer! Adjust the amount of green chilies and red chili powder according to your spice preference.

Dahi Wale Aloo (Potatoes in Yogurt Curry)

Ingredients:

- 4 medium-sized potatoes, peeled and cubed
- 1 cup plain yogurt (dahi)
- 2 tablespoons vegetable oil
- 1 teaspoon cumin seeds
- 1 teaspoon mustard seeds
- 1 onion, finely chopped
- 2 tomatoes, finely chopped or pureed
- 1 tablespoon ginger paste
- 1 tablespoon garlic paste
- 1 green chili, slit lengthwise
- 1/2 teaspoon turmeric powder
- 1/2 teaspoon red chili powder
- 1/2 teaspoon ground coriander
- Salt to taste
- Fresh coriander leaves for garnish

Instructions:

1. Boil the cubed potatoes until they are tender but still firm. Drain and set aside.
2. Whisk the plain yogurt in a bowl until smooth and set aside.
3. Heat vegetable oil in a large pan over medium heat.
4. Add cumin seeds and mustard seeds. Let them splutter.
5. Add chopped onions and sauté until they turn golden brown.
6. Add ginger paste, garlic paste, and green chili. Sauté for another minute until fragrant.
7. Add chopped tomatoes (or puree) to the pan. Cook until the tomatoes are soft and oil starts to separate from the mixture, about 5-7 minutes.
8. Add turmeric powder, red chili powder, ground coriander, and salt to the pan. Stir well to combine.
9. Add boiled potatoes to the pan. Mix gently with the spice mixture, ensuring the potatoes are coated evenly.
10. Reduce the heat to low and add whisked yogurt to the pan. Stir continuously to prevent curdling.

11. Simmer the curry for 5-7 minutes, stirring occasionally, until the potatoes are heated through and the yogurt is well incorporated.
12. Taste and adjust the seasoning if needed.
13. Garnish with fresh coriander leaves before serving.
14. Serve hot with rice or roti.

Enjoy your homemade Dahi Wale Aloo! Adjust the amount of green chili and red chili powder according to your spice preference.

Methi Malai Mutter (Fenugreek and Peas in Cream Sauce)

Ingredients:

- 1 cup fenugreek leaves (methi), washed and finely chopped
- 1 cup green peas (fresh or frozen)
- 1 tablespoon ghee or butter
- 1 onion, finely chopped
- 2 tomatoes, finely chopped or pureed
- 1 tablespoon ginger paste
- 1 tablespoon garlic paste
- 2 green chilies, slit lengthwise
- 1/4 cup cashew nuts, soaked in warm water for 30 minutes
- 1/2 cup milk
- 1/2 cup cream
- 1/2 teaspoon turmeric powder
- 1/2 teaspoon ground coriander
- 1/2 teaspoon red chili powder
- Salt to taste
- Fresh coriander leaves for garnish

Instructions:

1. Heat ghee or butter in a pan over medium heat.
2. Add chopped onions and sauté until golden brown.
3. Add ginger paste, garlic paste, and green chilies. Sauté for another minute.
4. Add chopped tomatoes (or puree) to the pan. Cook until the tomatoes are soft and oil starts to separate from the mixture, about 5-7 minutes.
5. Drain the soaked cashew nuts and transfer them to a blender or food processor. Add milk and blend into a smooth paste.
6. Add the cashew paste to the pan. Mix well with the onion-tomato mixture.
7. Add ground turmeric, ground coriander, red chili powder, and salt to the pan. Stir well to combine.
8. Add fenugreek leaves (methi) and green peas to the pan. Mix gently.
9. Cover the pan and cook on low heat for about 10 minutes, allowing the flavors to meld together and the vegetables to cook.
10. Add cream to the pan. Mix well and simmer for another 2-3 minutes.
11. Taste and adjust the seasoning if needed.

12. Garnish with fresh coriander leaves before serving.
13. Serve hot with rice, naan, or roti.

Enjoy your homemade Methi Malai Mutter! Adjust the amount of green chilies and red chili powder according to your spice preference.

Pindi Chole (Spicy Chickpea Curry)

Ingredients:

- 2 cups dried chickpeas (chole), soaked overnight and drained
- 2 tablespoons vegetable oil
- 2 onions, finely chopped
- 2 tomatoes, finely chopped or pureed
- 1 tablespoon ginger paste
- 1 tablespoon garlic paste
- 2 green chilies, slit lengthwise
- 1 teaspoon cumin seeds
- 2 teaspoons coriander powder
- 1 teaspoon dried pomegranate seeds (anardana)
- 1 teaspoon amchur (dried mango powder)
- 1/2 teaspoon turmeric powder
- 1/2 teaspoon red chili powder
- 1/2 teaspoon garam masala
- Salt to taste
- Fresh coriander leaves for garnish
- Lemon wedges for serving

Instructions:

1. Heat vegetable oil in a pressure cooker or large pot over medium heat.
2. Add cumin seeds and let them splutter.
3. Add chopped onions and sauté until golden brown.
4. Add ginger paste, garlic paste, and green chilies. Sauté for another minute until fragrant.
5. Add chopped tomatoes (or puree) to the pot. Cook until the tomatoes are soft and oil starts to separate from the mixture, about 5-7 minutes.
6. Add coriander powder, dried pomegranate seeds, amchur, turmeric powder, red chili powder, and salt to the pot. Stir well to combine.
7. Add soaked chickpeas to the pot. Mix well to coat the chickpeas with the spice mixture.
8. If using a pressure cooker, add about 3 cups of water. Close the lid and pressure cook for about 4-5 whistles, or until the chickpeas are tender.

9. If using a regular pot, add enough water to cover the chickpeas. Cover the pot and simmer on low heat for about 1.5 to 2 hours, or until the chickpeas are tender, stirring occasionally and adding more water if needed.
10. Once the chickpeas are cooked, sprinkle garam masala over the curry. Stir gently to combine.
11. Garnish with fresh coriander leaves before serving.
12. Serve hot with rice, naan, or roti.
13. Serve with lemon wedges on the side for squeezing over the curry, if desired.

Enjoy your homemade Pindi Chole! Adjust the amount of green chilies and red chili powder according to your spice preference.

Kofta Curry

Ingredients:

For the Koftas:

- 2 medium-sized potatoes, boiled and mashed
- 1 cup mixed vegetables (carrots, peas, beans), finely chopped and cooked
- 1/2 cup paneer, grated
- 2 tablespoons corn flour or chickpea flour
- 1 teaspoon ginger paste
- 1 teaspoon garlic paste
- 1/2 teaspoon garam masala
- Salt to taste
- Vegetable oil for frying

For the Curry:

- 2 tablespoons vegetable oil
- 1 onion, finely chopped
- 2 tomatoes, finely chopped or pureed
- 1 tablespoon ginger paste
- 1 tablespoon garlic paste
- 1 teaspoon cumin seeds
- 1 teaspoon coriander powder
- 1/2 teaspoon turmeric powder
- 1/2 teaspoon red chili powder
- 1/2 teaspoon garam masala
- Salt to taste
- Fresh coriander leaves for garnish

Instructions:

1. To make the koftas, mix together mashed potatoes, cooked mixed vegetables, grated paneer, corn flour or chickpea flour, ginger paste, garlic paste, garam masala, and salt in a bowl until well combined.
2. Shape the mixture into small round balls or oval-shaped koftas.

3. Heat vegetable oil in a deep frying pan over medium heat. Fry the koftas in batches until golden brown and crispy. Remove them from the oil and drain on paper towels. Set aside.
4. To make the curry, heat vegetable oil in a separate pan over medium heat.
5. Add cumin seeds and let them splutter.
6. Add chopped onions and sauté until golden brown.
7. Add ginger paste, garlic paste, and sauté for another minute until fragrant.
8. Add chopped tomatoes (or puree) to the pan. Cook until the tomatoes are soft and oil starts to separate from the mixture, about 5-7 minutes.
9. Add coriander powder, turmeric powder, red chili powder, garam masala, and salt to the pan. Stir well to combine.
10. Add water to adjust the consistency of the curry, if needed.
11. Gently add the fried koftas to the curry. Be careful not to break them.
12. Cover the pan and simmer on low heat for about 10-15 minutes to allow the flavors to meld together.
13. Taste and adjust the seasoning if needed.
14. Garnish with fresh coriander leaves before serving.
15. Serve hot with rice, naan, or roti.

Enjoy your homemade Kofta Curry! Adjust the amount of red chili powder according to your spice preference.